My First
Animal
Picture
Dictionary

Aa

amphibian

Amphibians begin life under water, but change as they grow, so they can breathe air and live on land, too.

animal

An **animal** is something that lives and moves around. Eagles, goldfish, spiders and rabbits are all animals.

albatross

Albatrosses are big sea birds that spend most of their life in the air.

ant

Ants are tiny insects that live together in big groups called colonies.

alligator

Alligators live in swamps and have long tails, short legs and fierce snapping jaws.

angelfish

Colourful **angelfish** often live in warm seas. Their flat body makes it hard for enemies to see them from the front.

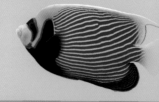

antelope

Antelopes are deer-like animals with long horns on their head.

antennae

Lots of insects have two **antennae** on their head to help them to smell and taste.

B b

antler

The horns on a male deer's head are called **antlers**.

ape

An **ape** looks like a monkey but has no tail.

baboon

Baboons are monkeys that live in big groups. They sleep sitting up to watch for danger.

badger

Badgers are night-time animals that eat small animals, fruit and worms.

bat

A **bat** is a small, furry night-time animal that looks like a mouse with wings. Bats hang upside down when they sleep.

beak

A **beak** is the hard part of a bird's mouth.

bear

A **bear** is a big, heavy animal with thick fur and sharp claws. Bears sleep for most of the winter.

bee

A **bee** is an insect with wings. Bees make honey.

beetle

A **beetle** is an insect with hard, shiny wing covers. Ladybirds are beetles.

bird

Birds have wings, feathers and a beak. Most birds can fly.

bison

Giant American **bison** live in herds on the grasslands of North America. Their shaggy coat keeps out the winter cold.

beaver

Beavers live in lakes and rivers and are good swimmers. They build dams in streams to make their homes.

bill

A bird uses its **bill** to eat, build a nest, and smooth its feathers.

boa constrictor

Boa constrictors are long snakes that wind themselves around their prey to squeeze it to death.

buffalo

Buffalo are large, cow-like animals that live in groups called herds. They have big horns.

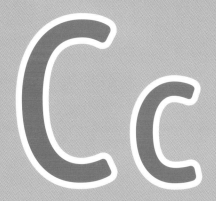

bull

A **bull** is a male animal of the cow family. Most bulls have horns.

calf

A **calf** is a young cow or bull. Calves drink milk for the first few months.

budgerigar

Budgerigars are small birds that live in big flocks in the wild. People often keep budgies as pets.

butterfly

A **butterfly** is an insect with four large wings.

camel

A **camel** is an animal with one or two humps on its back.

camouflage

Camouflage is when an animal hides from danger by blending in with the things around it.

cat

A **cat** is an animal with soft fur, sharp claws and a long tail. People keep small cats as pets. Lions and tigers are called big cats.

cattle

Cows, buffalo, and oxen are all kinds of **cattle**. Male cattle are bulls, females are cows and babies are calves.

caribou

Caribou is the North American name for reindeer. Caribou have antlers and live near the icy North Pole.

centipede

A **centipede** is a minibeast with lots of tiny legs.

caterpillar

A **caterpillar** looks like a worm with legs. It turns into a butterfly or moth.

chameleon

A **chameleon** is a lizard that lives in trees. Chameleons can change colour.

cheetah

Cheetahs are big wild cats, with spotted coats. They are the fastest runners in the world.

chicken

A **chicken** is a bird that farmers keep for eggs and meat. A male chicken is a cockerel and a female is a hen.

claw

A **claw** is the sharp, curved nail on the foot of a bird or animal.

chimpanzee

Chimpanzees are apes that live in big family groups. They eat and sleep in the trees.

cobra

A **cobra** is a kind of snake with poisonous fangs. One bite can kill.

chick

A **chick** is a baby bird.

chipmunk

Chipmunks are small, striped squirrels. They have a bushy tail and eat nuts.

cockerel

A **cockerel** is a male chicken.

cow

A **cow** is a large farm animal. People drink its milk.

crocodile

A **crocodile** is a reptile with sharp teeth, short legs and a long tail.

cockle

A **cockle** is a kind of shellfish that has two fan-like shells joined together.

coyote

Also called prairie wolves, **coyotes** live on the dry, grassy American plains.

crow

A **crow** is a big, black bird.

coral

Corals are tiny sea creatures. When some corals die, they leave a hard skeleton.

crab

Most **crabs** live in or near water and have a hard shell, eyes on stalks and big claws.

cub

Young lions, tigers, foxes and bears are called **cubs**.

Dd

dingo

A **dingo** is a wild dog from Australia.

dolphin

Dolphins are sea mammals. They have to hold their breath under water.

deer

Deer are shy animals that can run very fast. Male deer, called stags, have branched horns, or antlers. Female deer are called does, and the babies are fawns.

dog

A **dog** is an animal that barks. Dogs are often kept as pets. Foxes, jackals and wolves are wild dogs.

donkey

A **donkey** is a kind of small horse with long ears. Donkeys are used to carry people and things over rough paths.

a b c d e f g h i j k l m n o p q r s t u v w x y z

dragonfly

A **dragonfly** is a big flying insect that lives near water.

Ee

eel

An **eel** is a long, slimy, snake-like fish.

duck

A **duck** is a bird that lives near water. Ducks have waterproof feathers and webbed feet for swimming.

eagle

An **eagle** is a large bird with big wings, a curved beak and sharp claws for killing its prey.

egg

Birds, fish, snakes and lizards live inside **eggs** until they are big enough to hatch out.

duckling

A **duckling** is a young duck.

ears

Most animals have two **ears** on the top or side of their head for hearing sounds.

elephant

An **elephant** is a large, grey animal with big ears and a long trunk.

elephant seal

Elephant seals live in the freezing ocean near the South Pole.

elk

Also called red deer, **elk** live in American forests and have huge antlers.

eye

Animals have **eyes** to see with. Most animals have two eyes, but some, like spiders, have as many as eight!

Ff

feather

Birds have **feathers** on their body to keep them warm and dry. Wing feathers also help birds fly.

fish

A **fish** is a scaly animal that lives in water. Fish have gills for breathing under water.

flamingo

A **flamingo** is a tall, pink bird with very long legs for wading in water at the edge of lakes.

flock

A **flock** is a group of birds or sheep.

a b c d e f g h i j k l m n o p q r s t u v w x y z

fly

A **fly** is a small insect with one pair of wings. There are lots of different kinds of fly.

fox

A **fox** is a kind of wild dog with a long, bushy tail. Foxes hunt mainly at night.

Gg

foal

A **foal** is a young horse. Foals can stand up as soon as they are born. Young zebras and donkeys are also called foals.

frog

A **frog** is a small amphibian that lives in ponds and damp places. Some frogs live high in the treetops.

gazelle

Gazelles are long-legged antelopes that can run fast. They live in big herds on the grasslands of Africa. They have long, unbranched horns on their head.

fur

Fur is the thick, soft hair that covers some animals.

gerbil

A **gerbil** is a small animal with long, back legs and very soft fur. Children often keep gerbils as pets.

gibbon

Gibbons are small apes. They use their long arms to swing through the trees.

gills

Gills are the flaps of skin behind a fish's eye that let it breathe under water.

giraffe

A **giraffe** is a tall animal with long legs and a very long neck.

goat

Goats have long hair and horns.

goldfish

A **goldfish** is a small, golden-orange fish. People often keep pet goldfish.

goose

A **goose** is a large bird with a long neck that lives near water. A male goose is a gander, and a baby goose is a gosling.

Hh

gorilla

A **gorilla** is a strong, heavy ape with long arms for swinging in trees. Gorillas live in big family groups in African forests.

grasshopper

Grasshoppers are insects with strong back legs for jumping. They rub their back legs together to make a big noise.

guinea pig

A **guinea pig** is a small, furry animal with short legs and no tail.

hamster

A **hamster** is a small, furry animal with pockets inside its cheeks where it stores food.

gosling

A **gosling** is a young goose.

gull

Gulls are big birds that usually live near the sea. They catch fish with their long beak.

hare

A **hare** is like a big rabbit, with strong back legs and long ears.

hawk

A **hawk** is a bird of prey with sharp claws and a curved, pointed beak for catching and eating meat.

hen

A **hen** is a female chicken. Hens lay eggs.

heron

Herons are large birds that live near rivers and lakes. They have long legs for wading, and long, sharp beaks for catching fish.

herd

A **herd** is a big group of animals, such as zebras, buffalo, cows and deer.

hippopotamus

Hippopotamuses are big animals that love to wallow in muddy African rivers.

hedgehog

Hedgehogs are small, spiny night-time animals. When they are scared, they roll into a ball.

hoof

A **hoof** is the hard part of a horse's foot. Pigs and deer have hooves, too.

horn

Sheep, cattle and antelope have hollow **horns** for fighting other animals.

horse

A **horse** is a big animal with hooves. People ride horses and use them to pull heavy loads. Zebras and donkeys are kinds of horses.

hummingbird

Hummingbirds are tiny birds that sip sweet flower nectar through their long, pointed beak. They can hover in the air and even fly backwards.

hornbill

A **hornbill** is a bird with a big bill that has a kind of horn on top.

human

A **human** is a man, woman or child.

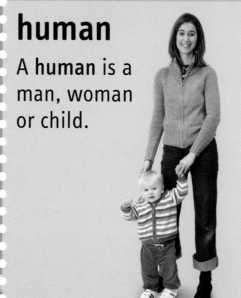

hyena

Hyenas are dog-like meat eaters that usually hunt at night.

Ii Jj Kk

iguana

An **iguana** is a large lizard that lives in trees in hot countries.

insects

An **insect** is a small animal with six legs. Many insects have wings. Butterflies, flies and beetles are all insects.

jaguar

A **jaguar's** spotted coat helps it hide from its prey in the forest.

jellyfish

Jellyfish are soft sea creatures with no bones, and stinging tentacles.

kangaroo

Kangaroos are big Australian animals with strong back legs for jumping.

kid

A **kid** is a young goat. Children are often called kids, too.

kitten

A **kitten** is a young cat.

Ll

leg

Animals need **legs** to get around. Some animals, like you, have only two legs, while others, like millipedes, have lots.

koala

Koalas are night-time animals from Australia that live, sleep and feed in eucalyptus trees.

ladybird

A **ladybird** is a small flying beetle. Most ladybirds are red with black spots.

lamb

A **lamb** is a young sheep that is still with its mother.

lemur

Lemurs live in big groups in forest on the island of Madagascar.

leopard

A **leopard** is a big wild cat with spots on its coat.

limpet

A **limpet** is a shellfish that looks like a tiny Chinese hat. Limpets stick to rocks under the sea.

llama

Llamas are camel-like animals with long fur.

lion

Lions are big wild cats that live on the African plains.

lobster

Lobsters live on the sea floor, where they hunt for food at night. They have eight legs and two sharp claws.

macaw

A **macaw** is a kind of parrot. Macaws have a strong, hooked beak for cracking open seeds and nuts.

lizard

A **lizard** is a reptile with a long body, four legs, scaly skin and a long tail.

lynx

A **lynx** is a wild cat with long legs, a short tail and tufted ears.

a b c d e f g h i j k l m n o p q r

mammal

A **mammal** is an animal that feeds its babies with its own milk. Mammals do not lay eggs and often have hair or fur on their body. Cats, goats, dolphins and people are all mammals.

mane

A **mane** is the long hair that grows on the back of the neck and head of animals like lions and horses.

mare

A **mare** is a female horse. Female zebras and donkeys are also called mares.

marsupial

Marsupials are mammals like koalas and kangaroos whose babies are born very young. The baby crawls to a pouch on its mother's tummy where it grows.

millipede

A **millipede** is a creature with lots of tiny legs. Millipede means "a thousand feet".

mole

Small, velvety **moles** have shovel-like front feet for digging tunnels in the ground.

mongoose

A **mongoose** is a small, fast, meat-eating animal that catches insects and lizards.

monkey

Monkeys have strong arms and long tails to swing from tree to tree.

moth

A **moth** is a night-time insect with four big wings. You often see moths fluttering around lights.

Nn

moose

A **moose** is the biggest kind of deer. Male moose have huge antlers, which they lose every autumn.

mouse

A **mouse** is a small, furry animal with a long tail. Mice have sharp front teeth for gnawing food.

nest

A **nest** is the home that animals like birds and mice make for their babies.

mussel

A **mussel** is a kind of shellfish that has two long oval shells that are joined together.

newt

Newts are lizard-like amphibians, which means they can breathe when they are in water and when they are out of it.

Oo

ostrich

Ostriches are the world's biggest birds and are bigger than a human. They cannot fly but are very fast runners.

owl

An **owl** is a bird that hunts for small animals at night. It has big eyes to help it see in the dark.

octopus

An **octopus** is a sea animal with a soft body and eight long arms.

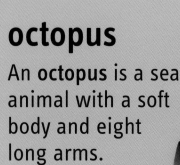

orang-utan

Orang-utans are big apes with reddish fur and long arms.

otter

Otters live near water and are very good swimmers with strong, webbed back feet.

oyster

An **oyster** is a shellfish that has two shells joined together. Pearls grow inside oyster shells.

Pp

parrot
A **parrot** is a bird with brightly coloured feathers and a sharp, curved beak for eating seeds. Some parrots can talk.

peacock
A **peacock** is a bird. Male peacocks can open out their beautiful tail feathers into a shimmering fan.

pack
A **pack** is a group of dogs or wolves that live and hunt together.

panda
Pandas look like big, black-and-white bears. Their favourite food is bamboo shoots.

paw
A **paw** is an animal's foot.

pelican
A **pelican** is a large, fish-eating bird with a big, pouched bill.

a b c d e f g h i j k l m n o p q r s t u v w x y z

penguin

A **penguin** is a black-and-white sea bird that lives in big colonies on cold, rocky coastlines. Penguins can't fly. Instead, they use their flipper-like wings for swimming after fish in the sea.

pheasant

Pheasants are big, often brightly coloured birds that like to run instead of fly.

pig

A **pig** is an animal with a fat body, short legs, and a short curly tail.

pigeon

A **pigeon** is a bird that makes a soft, cooing sound. Pigeons live in woods, towns and cities.

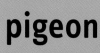

piglet

A **piglet** is a young pig.

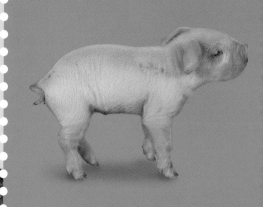

polar bear

A **polar bear** is a big, white bear that lives on the ice and snow near the North Pole.

pony

A **pony** is a small horse.

prey

Prey is any animal that is hunted and eaten by another animal.

puppy

A **puppy** is a young dog. Puppies love to chew things and can get into trouble!

porcupine

A **porcupine** has long spines. If it is attacked, it sticks its spines into its enemy.

puffin

A **puffin** is a sea bird with a short, curved beak. Puffins build nests in cliffs.

predator

A **predator** hunts and kills other animals for food.

puma

A **puma** is a big wild cat. It is also called a cougar, panther or mountain lion.

python

A **python** is a kind of snake that squeezes its prey to death.

a b c d e f g h i j k l m n o p q r s t u v w z

A B C D E F G H I J K L M N O P Q R S T U V W X Y Z

Rr

rat

Rats look like mice, but bigger. They will eat almost anything.

reindeer

Reindeer have antlers and live in the icy north.

rabbit

Small, furry **rabbits** have long ears and a fluffy white tail.

rattlesnake

A **rattlesnake** has a rattle on its tail, which it shakes when it is angry.

reptile

Reptiles have scaly skin and short legs, or no legs at all. Crocodiles, lizards, tortoises and snakes are all kinds of reptile. Reptiles lay eggs.

raccoon

A **raccoon** has a stripy tail and face markings that look like a mask.

ray

A **ray** is a flat fish with a long tail. Rays flap their fins like wings under water.

26

rhinoceros

A **rhinoceros** is a big animal with tough, leathery skin and horns on its head.

Ss

seal

Seals are sea animals with flippers for swimming. They hold their breath to swim under water.

salmon

A **salmon** is a kind of fish that lives in the sea but swims up rivers to lay its eggs.

sea lion

Sea lions live by the sea. They swim well but can also walk on land.

rodent

Rodents have two strong front teeth for gnawing. Mice, rats, gerbils and hamsters are all rodents.

scorpion

A **scorpion** has eight legs and a deadly sting at the end of its tail.

shark

A **shark** is a big fish. Some sharks have very sharp teeth and are fierce hunters.

a b c d e f g h i j k l m n o p q r s t u v w x y z

sheep

A **sheep** is an animal with a thick, woolly coat. Farmers raise sheep for their meat, wool and milk.

skin

The outer covering of an animal's body is its **skin**. Skin may be covered in fur, feathers or scales.

snake

A **snake** is a scaly reptile with a long body and no legs. Some snakes have a deadly bite.

shell

A **shell** is a hard covering around something. Shellfish have shells around them to protect their soft bodies.

slug

A **slug** has no bones and is like a snail with no shell. As slugs creep along, they leave a slimy trail.

spider

A **spider** is a minibeast with eight legs. Most spiders spin webs to catch insects for food.

shellfish

A **shellfish** is a soft-bodied animal that lives inside a shell. Some shellfish, like scallops, live between two shells.

snail

A **snail** is a small, soft animal that lives inside a spiral shell. Snails move slowly and leave a slimy trail.

sponge

Sponges are sea animals that feed on tiny animals and plants in the water.

squirrel

Small, furry **squirrels** live in trees. They have bushy tails and eat nuts.

starfish

A **starfish** is a star-shaped animal with five arms that lives in the ocean.

stag

A **stag** is a male deer. Stags have antlers.

stick insect

Stick insects are camouflaged to look just like the sticks and leaves where they live. They can even change colour.

tail

An animal's **tail** is the part that grows out from the end of its back.

stallion

A **stallion** is a male horse.

swan

A **swan** is a large bird with a long, curved neck. Swans live on rivers and lakes.

tapir

Tapirs live in forests. They have a short trunk for tearing leaves off branches.

terrapin

A **terrapin** is a small reptile with short legs and a shell on its back. Terrapins live in lakes, rivers and swamps.

toad

A **toad** is a small, frog-like amphibian that lives in ponds and damp places.

tree frog

Tree frogs live in trees. Suckers on their feet help them stick to the branches.

tiger

A **tiger** is a big, wild cat with orange fur and black stripes. Wild tigers are rare, but some still live in India and China.

tortoise

A **tortoise** is a slow-moving reptile with short legs and a big shell on its back.

turkey

Turkeys are large birds that nest on the ground. Farmers keep turkeys for their meat.

toucan

A **toucan** is a bird with black and white feathers. and a large bill.

turtle

A **turtle** is a reptile that lives in water. Turtles have short legs and a shell on their back.

U u V v W w

whale
A **whale** is a large sea animal. Unlike a fish, it breathes air through a blowhole on the top of its head.

udder
An **udder** is the part of a cow where the milk comes out to feed her calf.

walrus
A **walrus** is a fat, wrinkly sea animal. Walruses have whiskers and tusks.

wildebeest
Wildebeest are big antelopes that live in herds on the African plains. They are also called gnus.

vulture
A **vulture** is a big bird that eats dead animals.

wasp
A **wasp** is a flying insect with black and yellow stripes. Wasps have a sting.

wing
A **wing** is the part of an insect or bird that it uses for flying.

a b c d e f g h i j k l m n o p q r s t u v w x y z

wolf

A **wolf** is a kind of wild dog. Wolves live together in a big group called a pack.

Yy Zz

woodpecker

Woodpeckers have a sharp beak to peck out insects from bark.

zebra

A **zebra** looks like a horse with black and white stripes. Zebras live in Africa.

worm

A **worm** is a small, soft animal with a long body and no legs. Earthworms live in the ground.

yak

A **yak** is a large, cow-like animal with lots of shaggy hair and long horns.